EQUALITY

Created Equal in His Image

A Devotable Compilation Project

Copyright © 2020 by Devotable, LLC

Equality Created Equal in His Image
A 16 Week Devotional and Journal about Equality
www.devotableapp.com

ISBN (Paperback): 978-1-7349319-2-1

Devotable is a brand trying to reach the world with the Gospel of Jesus Christ.

We try to do three things through our platform. First, we want to encourage believers daily with insightful and powerful devotions. Second, we try to reach the lost through the power of daily scripture and devotion reading. Lastly, we spread the word of God around the world with technology.

In everything we do, this is our passion and mission.

If you want to learn more about us, connect with us, or be a part of our awesome movement, visit our website at

https://devotableapp.com

Table of Contents

EQUALITY

As we open our Bible and begin to read the very first chapter of Genesis, we discover all men and women are created equal in God's image. We are endowed with the same rights, afforded the same dignity, and designed with the same virtues by an all-powerful Maker. This thread of equality runs throughout the entirety of God's word and as Christians, we are continuously commanded to demonstrate those same values to others.

Diversity and equality are concepts easily talked about but not necessarily easy in practice. How do we love people we don't agree with? How do we care for and show respect to those who aren't like us? Our sin nature is skewed to show only those who look like us and think like us, favor. And while we may not like to admit prejudice is within us, it most certainly is. The fall of man brought sin and prejudice into the world.

As Christians, we are commanded to fight against this evil because we are all one people, all one race, created equal in God's image. We are commanded to show no partiality because God shows no partiality. We are required to pursue what is right according to what God's word teaches us, not according to what the world teaches.

We need to equip ourselves with the knowledge of God's word in order to combat the false teaching of racism, sexism, gender inequality, age discrimination, and other forms of bias that denies the rights God Himself has given to all humans.

All of these issues are the result of sin, and will never be solved outside of eternity in Heaven. However, we are still commanded to fight against such injustices in this fallen world and to do so, we need to be empowered by what God's word teaches. Perhaps even more importantly, we should teach younger generations about these problems and how to overcome them as well.

This devotional and journal is designed to be a thought-provoking and challenging study into what God's word has to say about such topics. It also challenges us, as a family, to have conversations about these subjects with our kids and talk about our responsibility as Christians relating to these topics.

In this devotional, let's learn about how we, as believers, are commanded to live out these truths of equality and diversity.

HOW TO USE THIS JOURNAL

Each week starts with a devotional. Read the devotional and accompanying Scripture to learn and challenge your perception of equality within the Christian life.

Each day of the week, there are questions relating to that week's devotion for adults and youth. The questions are designed to start conversations with you and your family about equality within race, gender, age, and other topics. They also encourage dialogue exploring how the Bible teaches us to behave and respond to those subjects.

Use those questions to help guide you and your family in self-reflection, biblical application, and spiritual growth.

Lastly, in the print versions, there are repetitive questions each day that everyone should be able to ask and answer relating to their life. Journal about prayer requests that are heavy on your soul, write and rejoice about requests that have been answered, and confess things you need to deal with.

As you continue with the journal, you'll be able to look back at the previous pages and see how things you were once praying about have been fulfilled. You'll get a better sense of how God is working through your life and how He is answering your prayers.

Often we pray for something and forget about it several weeks down the road. Journaling these things helps us remember just how good God is to always answer our prayers.

To obtain a copy of the journaling pages for free, please go to https://devotableapp.com/prayerjournalpages/

You can download a printable version of the devotional journal pages and keep up just like the physical book.

WEEK 1

Ruled by Peace

"Above all, put on love, which is the perfect bond of unity. And let the peace of Christ, to which you were also called in one body, rule your hearts. And be thankful." (Colossians 3:14-15)

Have you ever compared yourself or your circumstances to others? I know I have. The voice in my head says, "I wish I were more like…," or "I'm not as successful or respected as…" or "They have it all together, not like me." Sometimes the voice sounds more along the lines of, "I'm glad I'm not like…," or "They should try harder to make better choices as I do." Sound familiar?

When we compare ourselves to others, we fall into the enemy's trap of believing what I call "Ladder Lies." This is where we are ruled by the worldly perspective that we exist in a system of hierarchies, where some are above and some fall below, and the goal of life is to climb up and keep others down.

At their core, these lies are judgments. Whether we judge ourselves as inferior or superior, judgments are based on insecurity in who we are in Christ: existing on an equal plane with others as "heirs of God and co-heirs with Christ" (Romans 8:17). As Paul described, "There is no Jew or Greek, slave or free, male and female, since you are all one in Christ Jesus" (Galatians

3:28). Ladder Lies oppose the Kingdom's perspectives of equality and unity.

If we are not to judge (Matthew 7:1) or be ruled by worldly regulations (Colossians 2:20), what do we exchange for our Ladder Lies? Colossians 3:14 instructs us to, "Above all, put on love, which is the perfect bond of unity." When we look at others through Christ's loving eyes, we see ourselves as equal and unified. Comparing ourselves to others robs us of contentment. Ladder Lies are forms of idolatry that lead to anger, hatred, malice, and wrath. Knowing who we are in Christ and standing in equality and unity with others are the pathways to peace.

We are to "let the peace of Christ, to which you were also called in one body, rule your hearts. And be thankful" (Colossians 3:15). If God is the God of peace, as Paul calls Him, walking in His Spirit means allowing His peace to rule our hearts. We are not to focus on things we don't have or circumstances we didn't expect; instead, we are to focus on Christ's ongoing redemption and "give thanks in everything" (I Thessalonians 5:18).

When we release our judgments, the peace of God replaces those Ladder Lies, and the hierarchical ways of the world fade as our hearts are ruled by peace. We will then be "filled with all the fullness of God" (Ephesians 3:19).

Written By Donna E. Lane, Ph.D.

DAY ONE

ADULTS

What are some areas in your life where you have compared yourself to others? (consider both inferiority and superiority judgments)

_____
_____
_____
_____

Today I praise God for...

_____
_____
_____

Today I am confessing...

_____
_____
_____

Today I am praying for...

_____
_____
_____
_____

DAY ONE

YOUTH

When you compare yourself to your friends, how do you feel?

_____

_____

_____

Today I praise God for...

_____

_____

Today I am confessing...

_____

_____

Today I am praying for...

_____

_____

_____

DAY TWO

ADULTS

What does your "comparing voice" say in your thoughts? What are your "Ladder Lies"?

_____

_____

_____

_____

Today I praise God for...

_____

_____

Today I am confessing...

_____

_____

Today I am praying for...

_____

_____

_____

DAY TWO

YOUTH

Have you ever looked down on others? What were the reasons you did? How did you feel?

Today I praise God for...

Today I am confessing...

Today I am praying for...

DAY 3
PRAYER

Lord Jesus, cleanse my thoughts of all judgments of myself and others. Remove my Ladder Lies and all hierarchical perspectives, and help me to put on love. Allow me to see myself and others through Your eyes, not the eyes of the world. Fill me with your Holy

Spirit so my heart is ruled by peace. In Your holy name I pray, Amen.

"To bring about change, you must not be afraid to take the first step. We will fail when we fail to try."

ROSA PARKS

DAY FOUR

ADULTS

In what ways is your mind set on earthly things? In what ways is your mind focused on things above?

_____

_____

_____

_____

Today I praise God for...

_____

_____

_____

Today I am confessing...

_____

_____

_____

Today I am praying for...

_____

_____

_____

DAY FOUR

YOUTH

Have you ever felt put down by others? How did you respond? How did you feel?

_____

_____

_____

_____

Today I praise God for...

_____

_____

Today I am confessing...

_____

_____

Today I am praying for...

_____

_____

_____

DAY FIVE
ADULTS

What does it mean to be an heir of God and a co-heir with Christ? How does this knowledge produce peace?

Today I praise God for...

Today I am confessing...

Today I am praying for...

DAY FIVE
YOUTH

What do you think about the idea that you are a child of God?

_____

_____

_____

_____

Today I praise God for...

_____

_____

Today I am confessing...

_____

_____

Today I am praying for...

_____

_____

_____

_____

DAY SIX

ADULTS

If you saw yourself through Christ's eyes, what and who would you see? How would this perspective change how you see others?

Today I praise God for...

Today I am confessing...

Today I am praying for...

DAY SIX

YOUTH

What does the word "equality" mean to you?

_____

_____

_____

_____

Today I praise God for...

_____

_____

Today I am confessing...

_____

_____

Today I am praying for...

_____

_____

_____

WEEK 2

Seeking Equality among Multiple Generations within the Local Church

"Don't rebuke an older man, but exhort him as a father, younger men as brothers, older women as mothers, and the younger women as sisters with all purity." (1 Timothy 5:1-2)

We have all been in a place where we look to the younger or older generation with judgment and condescending thoughts within the church; although, one is not more important than another. The local church is supposed to be a place of unity surrounded by the gospel. However, generational conflict and strife between different age groups are as prominent as ever. Generations are separated within the local church, not having the opportunity to learn and grow under the wisdom and knowledge from each other. Or worse, there are churches where one cannot even find more than one or two generations represented within the congregation.

1 Timothy 5:1-2 gives a beautiful example of what it means to have unity and equality of age, and also, how we should treat all age groups within the local church. We are to treat and exhort (another word for encouragement) the older men

and women as parents, and we should look at the younger men and women in the church as siblings. Within the local church, we are committed to each other through membership, therefore we are committed to each other like a family. Paul instructed Timothy to close the gap of multiple generations to create equality and peace and to simply encourage the church to be family.

Each person of each age is important and is made in the image of God. This is important to remember when there is conflict between ages within the church. The 55+ group is not the church of the past, but they are the church. The children and youth groups are not the future of the church, but the church. The church should be a place of equality of all ages just as it is a place of equality of all races, nationalities, and languages. Each age group and generation brings a different perspective and gift to the local church, and that should be celebrated. Equality of age is a beautiful picture of the church and shows a necessary aspect that is needed to be a healthy and growing church.

Written By Faithe Bennett

DAY ONE

ADULTS

What ways do you think the local church displays inequality of ages?

_____

_____

_____

Today I praise God for...

_____

_____

Today I am confessing...

_____

_____

Today I am praying for...

_____

_____

DAY ONE
YOUTH

As a youth, what do you do in your local church?

Today I praise God for...

Today I am confessing...

Today I am praying for...

DAY TWO
ADULTS

Is there disunity within your local church? Why?

_____

_____

_____

_____

Today I praise God for...

_____

_____

Today I am confessing...

_____

_____

Today I am praying for...

_____

_____

_____

_____

DAY TWO
YOUTH

Do you see people of different ages not being kind to each other at church?

_____

_____

_____

_____

Today I praise God for...

_____

_____

Today I am confessing...

_____

_____

Today I am praying for...

_____

_____

_____

DAY 3
PRAYER

Father God, I thank You for the opportunity to be part of the Church and how there are multiple ages, generations, and paths of life that make it up. I thank You for the wisdom of those who are younger and older than I because they are gifted and equipped for the role You have given them. Lord, right now I pray that if there is any conflict or inequality within generations of the Church that You will cause repentance and peace. You have created each person for Your glory, and we will be careful to praise You. Amen.

"Every believer is commanded to be plugged in to a local church."

DAVID JEREMIAH

DAY FOUR

ADULTS

How do you view those of other generations in your church?

_____

_____

_____

_____

Today I praise God for...

_____

_____

Today I am confessing...

_____

_____

Today I am praying for...

_____

_____

_____

DAY FOUR

YOUTH

Do you talk with people, not in your Sunday school class, that are older or younger than you?

_____
_____
_____
_____

Today I praise God for...

_____
_____

Today I am confessing...

_____
_____

Today I am praying for...

_____
_____
_____

DAY FIVE
ADULTS

What are some ways you can promote unity and community between the older and younger generations?

_____

_____

_____

Today I praise God for...

_____

_____

_____

Today I am confessing...

_____

_____

_____

Today I am praying for...

_____

_____

_____

DAY FIVE
YOUTH

Would you want to learn and share time with other people not your age at church?

Today I praise God for...

Today I am confessing...

Today I am praying for...

DAY SIX
ADULTS

Have you ever thought about how each generation is the Church, not the future or the past? Explain your answer.

Today I praise God for...

Today I am confessing...

Today I am praying for...

DAY SIX
YOUTH

As a youth, how can you be a part of the Church?

_____

_____

_____

_____

Today I praise God for...

_____

_____

Today I am confessing...

_____

_____

Today I am praying for...

_____

_____

_____

_____

WEEK 3

Men and Women in Partnership

"Then God said, 'Let us make man in our image, according to our likeness. They will rule the fish of the sea, the birds of the sky, the livestock, the whole earth, and the creatures that crawl on the earth.' So God created man in his own image; he created him in the image of God; he created them male and female. God blessed them, and God said to them, 'Be fruitful, multiply, fill the earth, and subdue it. Rule the fish of the sea, the birds of the sky, and every creature that crawls on the earth.'"
(Genesis 1:26-28)

When God created Adam, he did not want him to be alone, so he created a partner for him. The word "partner" clearly denotes that God's true purpose was for the two to work together in all things. It is also very clear from reading in Genesis, that God gave dominion over all other living things on earth to both of them. Not just Adam. Just because there are differences in men and women, does not mean the scale is tipped in favor of or against either one. The differences are meant to complement each other. Equally does not necessarily mean identically. In Galatians 3:28, the Apostle Paul tells us, "There is no Jew or Greek, slave or free, male and female; since

you are all one in Christ Jesus.."

The Gospel of John, tells about a Samaritan woman who met Jesus at a well. We do not know her name, but we know of her past. After a conversation with Jesus, the woman went back to Samaria and told others about their meeting. Those people came to Christ because of her testimony. Jesus used her to minister and bring others to the Lord. When God places a calling on a person's life, why does it matter if that person is male or female? How can limitations be placed on women who are following a calling purposed by God? Just think of the many people the Samaritan woman brought to the Lord. And that's just one woman. There were many others in the Bible. Jesus wants all people to spread the good news, not just men and not just women--all people equally.

God says that a man and a woman are to become one. They are to make equal decisions and be a united front within their families. They should love each other, protect each other, raise their children together, work together, and worship together. In the Lord, woman is not independent of man, nor is man independent of woman. For as woman came from man, man also came through woman, and all things come from God.

Written By Gina Barton Sewell

DAY ONE

ADULTS

Do you have issues working with others of the opposite sex to further the Kingdom of God?

_____

_____

_____

_____

Today I praise God for...

_____

_____

_____

Today I am confessing...

_____

_____

_____

Today I am praying for...

_____

_____

_____

_____

DATE:

DAY ONE

YOUTH

Can you share the love of Jesus with a classmate, even if they aren't a boy or a girl like you are?

Today I praise God for...

Today I am confessing...

Today I am praying for...

41

DAY TWO
ADULTS

What are some examples of men and women who worked together in the Bible?

Today I praise God for...

Today I am confessing...

Today I am praying for...

DAY TWO

YOUTH

Can you think of some couples in the Bible who worked together to share the Good News?

_____

_____

_____

_____

Today I praise God for...

_____

_____

Today I am confessing...

_____

_____

Today I am praying for...

_____

_____

_____

DAY 3
PRAYER

Father God, help us
to realize God's
true purpose
for all of us,
no matter our
differences. Help
us to love and
honor each other in all
relationships. We are all
children of God and therefore
we all have a message to spread.
Give us the courage and boldness

DATE: ____________

to be a witness for You and not have feelings of inferiority or unworthiness. In Jesus' name. Amen

"Therefore what God has joined together, let no one separate."

MARK 10:9

DAY FOUR
ADULTS

Is there something you have wanted to do for the cause of Christ but didn't feel as if you were adequate?

Today I praise God for...

Today I am confessing...

Today I am praying for...

DAY FOUR
YOUTH

What are some ways you like to share Jesus with others?

_____

_____

_____

_____

Today I praise God for...

_____

_____

Today I am confessing...

_____

_____

Today I am praying for...

_____

_____

_____

DAY FIVE
ADULTS

Can you think of any verses in the Bible where we are encouraged to work together for a common cause?

_____
_____
_____
_____

Today I praise God for...

_____
_____
_____

Today I am confessing...

_____
_____
_____

Today I am praying for...

_____
_____
_____

DAY FIVE

YOUTH

Do you think God only wants boys/girls to share His Words? Or do you think He would like them to work together?

_____
_____
_____

Today I praise God for...

_____
_____

Today I am confessing...

_____
_____

Today I am praying for...

_____
_____
_____

DAY SIX
ADULTS

Have you ever felt that God couldn't use you because of your gender? Explain.

_____

_____

_____

_____

Today I praise God for...

_____

_____

_____

Today I am confessing...

_____

_____

_____

Today I am praying for...

_____

_____

_____

DAY SIX

YOUTH

Have you ever not invited someone to go to church with you because they were a boy/girl?

_____

_____

_____

Today I praise God for...

_____

_____

Today I am confessing...

_____

_____

Today I am praying for...

_____

_____

_____

WEEK 4
Unity in Christ

"There is one body and one Spirit—just as you were called to one hope at your calling—one Lord, one faith, one baptism, one God and Father of all, who is above all and through all and in all."
(Ephesians 4:4-6)

In local churches, there are various traditions used to bring about unity. Some for example find unity in being a traditional church, being old fashioned, having hymnals, sitting in chairs, not compromising beliefs, in being a branded church, etc. It is important to have unity, but that unity must be rooted in something that is completely unifying. In the text above, Paul is talking about unity in the body. Notice Paul does not say unity is found in things or identity markers; instead, he says unity is found in Christ and that it leads to spiritual maturity. There are a few different reasons found in the text as to why Christ brings unity in the church.

The moment a local church unites on anything that isn't Jesus is the moment when they start to go off course. That is the point where the church will not be able to work together and that is when the body doesn't grow. Jesus calls people of

all backgrounds, ages, and ethnicities to the church. Jesus gave every person in the church the gift of salvation, and He gives each church what it needs to function.

In the church there is only one faith. The church was composed of regenerated people who were brought to faith in Christ. Christ is the object of our faith. Every single person in a church may not be at the same level of spiritual maturity, but every single person in the church is equal in having faith. This faith in Christ is what every believer has in common. There is only one faith in the church, and that faith's object is Jesus Christ.

Some Christians get swept about by every single wave of doctrine. Different movements and organizations have underlying differences. The church sometimes over-corrects on doctrine by centering on something that is not found in Scripture, church history, and implication of the gospel. The church of Ephesus was told that until they attained unity of the faith people would be blown around by every wind of doctrine. The church is being tossed about today and will be until the church is unified in the faith that is found in Jesus Christ.

Written By Nicholas Tim Murphy

DAY ONE
ADULTS

What do you think is the meaning of unity? Do you see that in your own life?

_____

_____

_____

_____

Today I praise God for...

_____

_____

Today I am confessing...

_____

_____

Today I am praying for...

_____

_____

_____

DAY ONE
YOUTH

What brings the church together?

_____

_____

_____

Today I praise God for...

_____

_____

Today I am confessing...

_____

_____

Today I am praying for...

_____

_____

_____

DAY TWO

ADULTS

How can you be an agent of unity in the church?

Today I praise God for...

Today I am confessing...

Today I am praying for...

DAY TWO

YOUTH

Can anything bring people together the way Jesus brings people together?

_____

_____

_____

_____

Today I praise God for...

_____

_____

Today I am confessing...

_____

_____

Today I am praying for...

_____

_____

_____

_____

DAY 3
PRAYER

Heavenly Father, the
world does not
have unity. The
church doesn't
have unity. True
unity is found
in the gospel. I
pray that the church
would become unified
in the gospel alone so we
can demonstrate unity to a lost
world. In Jesus' name, Amen.

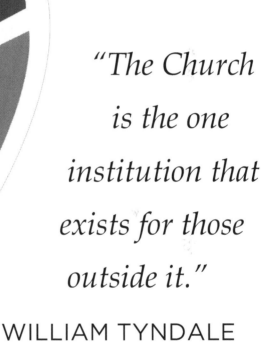

*"The Church
is the one
institution that
exists for those
outside it."*

WILLIAM TYNDALE

DATE:

DAY FOUR
ADULTS

How can you be an agent of unity in your community?

Today I praise God for...

Today I am confessing...

Today I am praying for...

DAY FOUR

YOUTH

How does Jesus bring people together?

_____

_____

_____

_____

Today I praise God for...

_____

_____

Today I am confessing...

_____

_____

Today I am praying for...

_____

_____

_____

DAY FIVE
ADULTS

Why is biblical unity important?

_____

_____

_____

_____

Today I praise God for...

_____

_____

_____

Today I am confessing...

_____

_____

_____

Today I am praying for...

_____

_____

_____

DAY FIVE

YOUTH

Is Jesus all that is needed to bring people together?

_____

_____

_____

Today I praise God for...

_____

_____

Today I am confessing...

_____

_____

Today I am praying for...

_____

_____

_____

_____

DAY SIX
ADULTS

How can you model biblical unity?

Today I praise God for...

Today I am confessing...

Today I am praying for...

DAY SIX
YOUTH

What is your favorite thing about being around other people united by Jesus and why?

_____
_____
_____

Today I praise God for...

_____
_____
_____

Today I am confessing...

_____
_____
_____

Today I am praying for...

_____
_____
_____

WEEK 5

Practicing for Heaven

"Again, truly I tell you, if two of you on earth agree about any matter that you pray for, it will be done for you by my Father in heaven. For where two or three are gathered together in my name, I am there among them."
(Matthew 18:19-20)

We moved to Japan when I was four years old. My father, a U.S. Marine, had previously served in the Middle East and Viet Nam. This was our first overseas adventure as a family.

"Our neighbors will be Japanese," Mom said. "God makes us different." She said we were privileged to live among beautifully distinct new neighbors.

Mom embraced Japan. She dragged the family all over in trains and buses. We camped on Mt. Fuji. We dug for clams in the bay alongside our Japanese neighbors.

Dad's next orders brought us to San Diego. Mrs. Clark was my new fifth grade teacher. In her class, I learned about slavery. She read an abridged version of Roots by African-American author Alex Haley. He recounts his family history from Gambia, Africa to America. The story horrified me. The abduction, transport, and enslavement of free-born Kunta Kinte, Haley's ancestor, was shackled to the hull of a slave ship stuffed with other men, women, and children. At 10, I was devastated to learn this was

how the world worked. "There is no way this is how God wants things to be," I remember telling my mother.

"Men can be very cruel," my mother said. "You must make every effort to love others even if it seems you're the only one doing it. This is difficult, but it matters."

In the verse above, we get a glance at heaven's diverse human population. The word "nations" is translated into English from the Greek word ethnos like our word "ethnic." Every human ethnic group is represented.

The mission of the Church is to build a new culture that reflects God's love and goodness. This is our task as people reconciled to God. This is why Jesus taught His disciples to pray: "Your Kingdom come, Your will be done, on earth as it is in Heaven" (Matthew 6:10). Jesus expects the Kingdom of God to invade our world through those who pray His words.

Jesus gives His vision for human relationships in Matthew 18:18. "Whatever you loose on earth will have been loosed in heaven."

In Matthew 18, Jesus teaches about justice and equality, the outcome of human relationships made right. The results echo into eternity.

Here's the challenge: practice makes perfect. Do what Jesus teaches in Matthew 18. Get good at these and we'll be better prepared, now and in the future, for living in God's everlasting Kingdom.

Written By Bryon Mondok

DAY ONE

ADULTS

Read Matthew 18:1-5. What is it about children that Jesus thinks is important for adults to have on display in their lives?

_____

_____

_____

Today I praise God for...

_____

_____

Today I am confessing...

_____

_____

Today I am praying for...

_____

_____

_____

DAY ONE
YOUTH

What are some differences between grown-ups and kids Jesus may be teaching about?

_____

_____

_____

_____

Today I praise God for...

_____

_____

_____

Today I am confessing...

_____

_____

_____

Today I am praying for...

_____

_____

_____

_____

69

DAY TWO
ADULTS

Read Matthew 18:6-9. How seriously do we need to take Jesus' warnings about how children and others should be treated?

Today I praise God for...

Today I am confessing...

Today I am praying for...

DAY TWO

YOUTH

How does Jesus want us to treat people who are weaker than us?

_____

_____

_____

_____

Today I praise God for...

_____

_____

Today I am confessing...

_____

_____

Today I am praying for...

_____

_____

_____

DAY 3
PRAYER

*Lord, please open
my eyes to how
I can make
relationships in
my life look like
the relationship
You want to have
with me. May I live
the kind of life where it
is easy for Your Kingdom
to invade the everyday world
around me.*

DATE:

*"You must make
every effort to
love others even
if it seems you're
the only one doing
it. This is difficult, but
it matters."*

SUSAN B. MONDOK

73

DAY FOUR
ADULTS

Read Matthew 18:10-14. How important to Jesus is the life of one person?

_____

_____

_____

Today I praise God for...

_____

_____

Today I am confessing...

_____

_____

Today I am praying for...

_____

_____

_____

DAY FOUR
YOUTH

Who sees everything that happens to children?

_____
_____
_____

Today I praise God for...

_____
_____

Today I am confessing...

_____
_____

Today I am praying for...

_____
_____
_____

DAY FIVE
ADULTS

Read Matthew 18:15-17. What is Jesus' mission for relationships in these verses? Being heard? Treating someone as an outcast?

_____

_____

_____

_____

Today I praise God for...

_____

_____

_____

Today I am confessing...

_____

_____

_____

Today I am praying for...

_____

_____

_____

DAY FIVE
YOUTH

What does it mean to "win a brother?" Does Jesus want us to win an argument, or is there another kind of prize He wants us to win?

_____

_____

_____

Today I praise God for...

_____

_____

Today I am confessing...

_____

_____

Today I am praying for...

_____

_____

_____

DAY SIX

ADULTS

Read Matthew 18:18-20. What do "binding" and "loosing" mean? How might actions here impact heaven for somebody else?

Today I praise God for...

Today I am confessing...

Today I am praying for...

DAY SIX

YOUTH

Why is it important for those who follow Jesus to pray and agree on things together?

Today I praise God for...

Today I am confessing...

Today I am praying for...

WEEK 6

One Man-One Blood

"From one man he has made every nationality to live over the whole earth." (Acts 17:26)

There it was in front of my eyes: the spot on the census form asking for my race. I was thankful to see an option marked other. I gladly chose that option and filled in the word "human" where it asked me to specify.

Where did this idea of separate races come from? Certainly not from Scripture! Paul couldn't have said it more clearly: we come from one man—one blood.

We are one race; the human race. Why is that so hard to grasp?

Perhaps we're more influenced by Darwin than we realize. It was Darwin who divided humanity into distinct races and was convinced that the white race was more advanced than the black race.[1] It was Darwin who wrote that in the future, "the civilized races of man will...exterminate and replace...the savage races."[2]

In God's eyes, we are not multiple races. There is no white race or black race. And yet Darwin's words help us to see the dark strategy behind the curtain, which is very simply to divide and conquer. God's very first command to our first parents, Adam and Eve, was to "fill the earth and subdue it" (Genesis 1:28). Racism causes us to subdue one another.

In short, racism is based on a fraudulent lie that leads to self-destruction.

To combat our rush into the abyss, God raised up Abraham to form a nation through whom "all the peoples on the earth will be blessed" (Genesis 12:3). The ultimate fulfillment of this promise came through the Jewish Messiah, Jesus.

But even He didn't come in the package expected of Him. When He appeared, He was not recognized for Who He is. You see, He did not have the expected religious pedigree. He came from the wrong side of the tracks. He hung out with the despised and destitute. And — horror of horrors — he reached out to dirty, stinky Gentiles!

For this reason, the religious people hated not only Him but also His herald to the Gentiles. Even though Paul was one of them, they were determined to kill him. Why? Because of his commission to reach the Gentiles (Acts 22:21).

Somehow they'd forgotten they were stewards — not owners — of God's Kingdom.

What about us today? As Jesus-followers who are tasked with Kingdom stewardship, how are we doing? Maybe we don't stone others or wear white-hooded sheets. But do we secretly harbor feelings of "superiority" toward those of a different race, theology, socioeconomic status, or political stripe? Are we willing to concede equal status toward those who are not like us?

Written By Gary David Flamberg

DAY ONE
ADULTS

How does the Bible dismantle the myth of multiple races?

_____

_____

_____

Today I praise God for...

_____

_____

Today I am confessing...

_____

_____

Today I am praying for...

_____

_____

_____

DAY ONE
YOUTH

How does God feel about racism?

_____

_____

_____

_____

Today I praise God for...

_____

_____

Today I am confessing...

_____

_____

Today I am praying for...

_____

_____

_____

_____

DAY TWO

ADULTS

How does racism lead to self-destruction?

_____
_____
_____
_____

Today I praise God for...

_____
_____
_____

Today I am confessing...

_____
_____
_____

Today I am praying for...

_____
_____
_____

DAY TWO

YOUTH

How does racism hurt all people?

_____
_____
_____
_____

Today I praise God for...

_____
_____
_____

Today I am confessing...

_____
_____
_____

Today I am praying for...

_____
_____
_____
_____

DAY 3
PRAYER

LORD, may we
never forget
that we all come
from one blood —
and that we who
follow You are
saved by one blood.
May this truth — and all
of its ramifications — burn
deep in our beings.

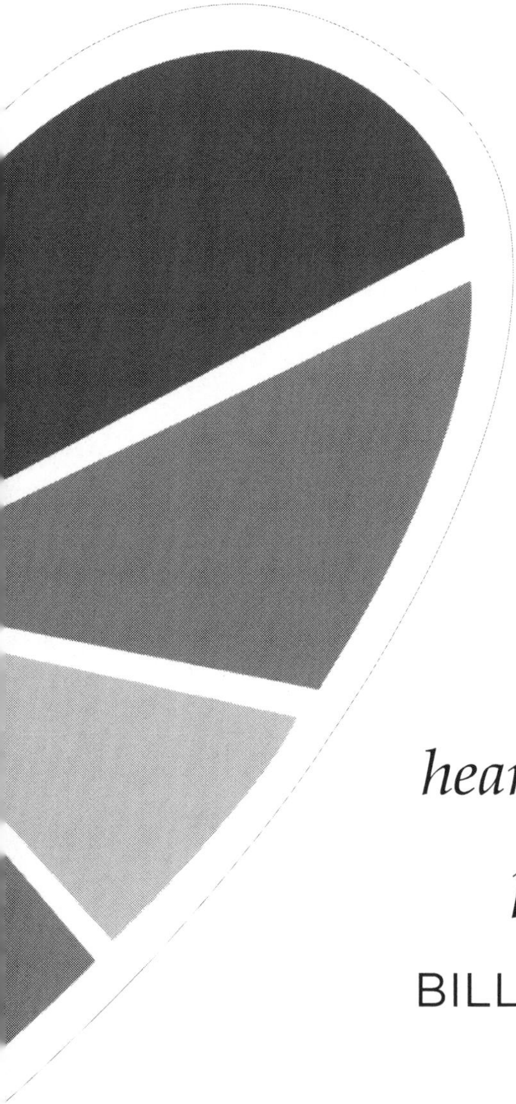

"Racial or ethnic prejudice is a sin in the eyes of God, and no Christian should allow his or her heart to be filled with prejudice."

BILLY GRAHAM

DAY FOUR
ADULTS

How has your thinking been skewed by racism?

_____

_____

_____

_____

Today I praise God for...

_____

_____

_____

Today I am confessing...

_____

_____

_____

Today I am praying for...

_____

_____

_____

DAY FOUR

YOUTH

How have you been hurt by racism?

_____

_____

_____

Today I praise God for...

_____

_____

Today I am confessing...

_____

_____

Today I am praying for...

_____

_____

_____

DATE:

DAY FIVE
ADULTS

How did Jesus combat racism?

Today I praise God for...

Today I am confessing...

Today I am praying for...

DAY FIVE

YOUTH

In what way was Jesus a good example for us on treating people who are different than us?

Today I praise God for...

Today I am confessing...

Today I am praying for...

DAY SIX
ADULTS

What steps does the church need to take to address racism?

_____

_____

_____

_____

Today I praise God for...

_____

_____

_____

Today I am confessing...

_____

_____

_____

Today I am praying for...

_____

_____

_____

_____

DAY SIX

YOUTH

How can you behave toward those who are different from you?

_____

_____

_____

Today I praise God for...

_____

_____

Today I am confessing...

_____

_____

Today I am praying for...

_____

_____

_____

WEEK 7

Neighborly Love

"My brothers and sisters, do not show favoritism as you hold on to the faith in our glorious Lord Jesus Christ." (James 2:1)

The COVID-19 pandemic of 2020 was hard for all of us. For those who suffered from the virus or lost a loved one because of it, life was very grim. We were also getting caught up in a battle of opinions and perspectives, forgetting to love one another.

It saddens me to watch people on opposite sides of issues disrespecting each other just because their perspectives do not match. If we cannot love like Jesus and serve others during a pandemic, how can we expect to be effective afterward?

If we are trying to cultivate genuine faith and become Christ-like, we cannot judge others based on appearance, social status, wealth, education, and opinions. We must love unconditionally.

We are not perfect. Humans are born with a sinful nature. This nature predetermines we will be impressed with things we can see, such as wealth, education, fame, and beauty. Thus, we tend to discount the needs of those who do not have visually appealing lives: poor, uneducated, or unsuccessful.

James reminds us that attitudes of favoritism are sinful because we are commanded to love one another. "Indeed, if you fulfill the royal law prescribed in the Scripture, Love your neighbor as

yourself, you are doing well"(James 2:8).

Genuine, unconditional love is giving selflessly, putting the needs of others ahead of our own, showing the love of Jesus to our neighbors. Jesus is not referring to just the people living with us or in our neighborhood. He is referring to everybody! We are commanded to love ALL people earnestly.

"Since you have purified yourselves by your obedience to the truth, so that you show sincere brotherly love for each other, from a pure heart love one another constantly." (1 Peter 1:22).

There are some people we just don't like, right? But, as Christians, through love in Jesus, we can love those people too.

God loved us so much that He gave His Son, Jesus, to die for our sins. The gift of salvation is available to everyone because God is impartial. When we accept His perfect love and forgiveness, our self-absorption diminishes and we become more sensitive to the needs of others.

A born-again child of God has the power, through the Holy Spirit, to love others sacrificially as Jesus loves us. It is a power that expounds from the believer loving God with all his heart and mind.

Every believer will live in heaven with Jesus. He has gone to prepare our home. He WILL return and take us home (John 14:1-3). The only requirement of eternal citizenship is salvation through Jesus; not our financial statement or our resume.

Stop the hate and partiality! Instead, share the love of Jesus to everyone.

Written By Crystal A. Dixon

DAY ONE

ADULTS

Does our eternal life depend on our success?

_____

_____

_____

Today I praise God for...

_____

_____

Today I am confessing...

_____

_____

Today I am praying for...

_____

_____

_____

DAY ONE
YOUTH

Does God show favoritism?

Today I praise God for...

Today I am confessing...

Today I am praying for...

DAY TWO

ADULTS

Have you ever found yourself on the receiving end of prejudicial judgments? How did it feel?

Today I praise God for...

Today I am confessing...

Today I am praying for...

DAY TWO

YOUTH

Is it possible to love someone we really don't like? Explain.

_____

_____

_____

_____

Today I praise God for...

_____

_____

Today I am confessing...

_____

_____

Today I am praying for...

_____

_____

_____

_____

DAY 3
PRAYER

Heavenly Father, thank You for loving us and for sending Your Son, Jesus, to save us from our sins. Lord, guide us in loving others. We pray for strength and passion to rekindle and share Your love, causing ripple effects across Your lands, so that hate may diminish and love is raised. In Jesus' name, Amen.

"None are more unjust in their judgments of others than those who have a high opinion of themselves."

CHARLES SPURGEON

DAY FOUR
ADULTS

Have you ever conveyed or thought prejudicial judgments against others? How did it feel?

_____

_____

_____

_____

Today I praise God for...

_____

_____

_____

Today I am confessing...

_____

_____

_____

Today I am praying for...

_____

_____

_____

DAY FOUR

YOUTH

For whom did Jesus die? Why?

Today I praise God for...

Today I am confessing...

Today I am praying for...

DAY FIVE
ADULTS

How can you rekindle and share the love of Jesus in your community?

_____

_____

_____

_____

Today I praise God for...

_____

_____

_____

Today I am confessing...

_____

_____

_____

Today I am praying for...

_____

_____

_____

DAY FIVE

YOUTH

If you disagree with someone's opinion, does it matter if you are kind to them or not?

_____

_____

_____

Today I praise God for...

_____

_____

Today I am confessing...

_____

_____

Today I am praying for...

_____

_____

_____

DAY SIX
ADULTS

How can you cultivate an impartial and unconditional, Christ-like love in your home?

_____

_____

_____

_____

Today I praise God for...

_____

_____

_____

Today I am confessing...

_____

_____

_____

Today I am praying for...

_____

_____

_____

DAY SIX
YOUTH

Is it okay for us to decide what groups of people to love or not love? Why?

_____
_____
_____
_____

Today I praise God for...

_____
_____

Today I am confessing...

_____
_____

Today I am praying for...

_____
_____
_____

WEEK 8

No Partiality

"Then Peter began to speak: 'Now I truly understand that God doesn't show favoritism, but in every nation the person who fears him and does what is right is acceptable to him.'"
(Acts 10:34-35)

After recent events in the United States, I needed to read this Scripture and allow it to settle within my spirit as a reminder of how God feels about His people. As an African American woman working in a professional world where, in almost all settings, I am considered a "minority," I felt Peter's words sharpen me as iron encouraging me to persevere in the most racially, politically, and economically charged environment I have ever experienced.

I would have never imagined the start of a new decade would fuel a sense of reverse thinking. I imagined this year being more about vision and forward progression, but unfortunately, I see veiled blindness and systemic oppression. Many times I find myself asking the question, "How did we get here?"

In this verse, Peter reveals that with God there is no

partiality, which tells us there were those who did not believe this. If this was occurring so many years ago with a different group of individuals, I wondered if it is our time as the Church to remind others there is no prejudice in God.

"How can we do this, Lord?" I prayed. In my mind I saw the words, "Through our actions." If there is no partiality, favoritism, bias, or prejudice with our Heavenly Father who created us, then where did we get the notion this should ever exist in the first place? The enemy, also known as the great deceiver. This is so apropos during this season where the love of many has waxed cold, lawlessness abounds, and hearts are hardened.

Then I remembered who we as the body of Christ belong to and how He feels about us. As we are still battling the decisions of those who came before, let us not forget how our Creator feels about us. He even came to ensure we are all set free. He did not save His salvation for one race, creed, or political party. He came for all, but we must love and believe.

As we continue to grow deeper and stronger in God, let us put the Word to work and literally be the hands and feet of Jesus. Let us rise to the standard of equality, and let it start with the actions of you and me.

Written By Dr. Natalie H. Ragland

DAY ONE

ADULTS

How can you be intentional about your own perception of bias?

_____

_____

_____

_____

Today I praise God for...

_____

_____

_____

Today I am confessing...

_____

_____

_____

Today I am praying for...

_____

_____

_____

DAY ONE
YOUTH

What can you learn from this devotional?

_____
_____
_____
_____

Today I praise God for...

_____
_____
_____

Today I am confessing...

_____
_____
_____

Today I am praying for...

_____
_____
_____
_____

DATE:

DAY TWO
ADULTS

How will you apply this Bible selection in the coming days?

Today I praise God for...

Today I am confessing...

Today I am praying for...

DAY TWO

YOUTH

Why do you think it is important for us to be unbiased?

_____

_____

_____

_____

Today I praise God for...

_____

_____

Today I am confessing...

_____

_____

Today I am praying for...

_____

_____

_____

_____

DAY 3
PRAYER

*Heavenly Father,
protect us. Be our
Guide through
this wilderness
and valley. Heal
our land and help
us to persevere; to
not grow weary in
well-doing, and seek You
first. Let us be mindful of
our actions, our thoughts, and
our walk. Give us the courage to*

be bold, but provide us with the sensitivity to recognize where we fall short. We are so grateful there is no bias with You and let us use You as an example for the way we should live our fleeting lives each day. In Jesus' name, Amen.

DATE:

DAY FOUR
ADULTS

Do you know someone who needs to hear these words?

_____

_____

_____

_____

Today I praise God for...

_____

_____

_____

Today I am confessing...

_____

_____

_____

Today I am praying for...

_____

_____

_____

DAY FOUR

YOUTH

Have you ever felt like someone treated you differently? How did that make you feel?

Today I praise God for...

Today I am confessing...

Today I am praying for...

DAY FIVE

ADULTS

How can you be the hands and feet of Jesus?

Today I praise God for...

Today I am confessing...

Today I am praying for...

DAY FIVE
YOUTH

How can you use this Bible verse in your life today?

_____

_____

_____

_____

Today I praise God for...

_____

_____

Today I am confessing...

_____

_____

Today I am praying for...

_____

_____

_____

DAY SIX

ADULTS

What change can you make today to be unbiased?

_____

_____

_____

_____

Today I praise God for...

_____

_____

_____

Today I am confessing...

_____

_____

_____

Today I am praying for...

_____

_____

_____

DAY SIX

YOUTH

What does being the hands and feet of Jesus mean to you?

_____
_____
_____
_____

Today I praise God for...

_____
_____
_____

Today I am confessing...

_____
_____
_____

Today I am praying for...

_____
_____
_____

WEEK 9

Everybody, Always

"I give you a new command: Love one another. Just as I have loved you, you are also to love one another." (John 13:34)

"I love you!" my youngest daughter said earnestly, attempting to make up with her sister after a recent squabble. "I love you, too," my oldest replied somewhat reluctantly, "except when you do that!" Can you relate?

As believers in Christ, we are called to love everyone—no exceptions. But in reality, it's not always that straightforward. As the saying goes, "No one ever said love was easy. And if they did, they lied." (Jenn Sterling)

Human beings are inherently sinful and fundamentally flawed with the capacity to frustrate, anger, baffle, and deeply wound one another. We are a wonderfully rich and diverse species, yet those differences can be a source of much confusion, conflict, and division between us. From the way we look, speak, and live out our beliefs and values, to our cultural experiences, educational backgrounds, and even our zip codes, each person brings their own unique contribution to the table—and some of it may be more palatable to us than others.

No, loving others is never easy, but Jesus calls us to do it

anyway. Why? Because He does.

Male and female, rich and poor, healthy and sick, honorable and dishonorable; Jesus did not discriminate. Instead, He demonstrated a radical, passionate, counter-cultural love to each and every person He encountered — without strings, without judgment, and without exception. A redeeming love that pointed people toward the Father and offered hope and freedom to a world that was weary, broken, and lost. A self-sacrificial love that took Him all the way to the cross. A love that is still very much evident today.

And we, as undeserving recipients of this abundant, life-changing love, have a responsibility to extend it to those around us, so that, as Jesus said, "By this everyone will know that you are my disciples…" (John 13:35).

As ambassadors for Christ, our love for one another should be the hallmark of our ministry as we seek to live out our calling and bring the Good News to the people that God has placed in our path. All the people — no matter how difficult or uncomfortable it may be.

Bob Goff writes, "Every time I wonder who I should love and for how long I should love them, God continues to whisper to me: Everybody, always."

Let this be our call to action today. To love like Jesus — everybody, always.

Written By Vicki Bentley

DAY ONE
ADULTS

How would you describe Jesus' love toward you personally?

_____

_____

_____

_____

Today I praise God for...

_____

_____

_____

Today I am confessing...

_____

_____

_____

Today I am praying for...

_____

_____

_____

DAY ONE
YOUTH

What do you think it means to love everybody, always?

_____

_____

_____

_____

Today I praise God for...

_____

_____

_____

Today I am confessing...

_____

_____

_____

Today I am praying for...

_____

_____

_____

DAY TWO

ADULTS

Think of specific people or groups you find difficult to love. How can you ask God to help you overcome these barriers.

_____

_____

_____

_____

Today I praise God for...

_____

_____

_____

Today I am confessing...

_____

_____

_____

Today I am praying for...

_____

_____

_____

_____

DATE:

DAY TWO

YOUTH

How did Jesus show love to the people He met every day during His ministry on earth?

Today I praise God for...

Today I am confessing...

Today I am praying for...

127

DAY 3
PRAYER

Lord Jesus, thank You for the abundant love and endless grace that You have lavished upon each one of us. Help us to look to Your example as we seek to share that love with the people You have placed in our path today — without exception.

Amen.

"Every time
I wonder who
I should love
and for how
long I should love
them, God continues
to whisper to me:
Everybody, always."

BOB GOFF

DAY FOUR
ADULTS

What does Jesus' example teach us about how we can better interact with and love challenging people in our life?

_____

_____

_____

_____

Today I praise God for...

_____

_____

_____

Today I am confessing...

_____

_____

_____

Today I am praying for...

_____

_____

_____

DAY FOUR

YOUTH

Think of people that you find hard to love. How can Jesus' example help you to love them anyway?

_____

_____

_____

_____

Today I praise God for...

_____

_____

Today I am confessing...

_____

_____

Today I am praying for...

_____

_____

_____

DAY FIVE

ADULTS

Would you consider yourself a person known by your love for others? If not, consider how you can take steps to change this.

_____

_____

_____

Today I praise God for...

_____

_____

Today I am confessing...

_____

_____

Today I am praying for...

_____

_____

_____

DAY FIVE

YOUTH

By showing love to others, what are you teaching them about Jesus?

_____

_____

_____

Today I praise God for...

_____

_____

Today I am confessing...

_____

_____

Today I am praying for...

_____

_____

_____

DAY SIX
ADULTS

What are some steps you can take this week to "love like Jesus?"

_____

_____

_____

_____

Today I praise God for...

_____

_____

Today I am confessing...

_____

_____

Today I am praying for...

_____

_____

_____

DAY SIX

YOUTH

Think of some different ways you can show love to people in your life this week.

_____
_____
_____
_____

Today I praise God for...

_____
_____

Today I am confessing...

_____
_____

Today I am praying for...

_____
_____
_____

WEEK 10

Love and Peacemaking in Relationships

"Pursue peace with everyone, and holiness—without it no one will see the Lord."
(Hebrews 12:14)

How do we show love and how can we be a peacemaker in our relationships? We love others and bring peace to our relationships when we follow what is true and do good.

God's Word has a lot to say about how to treat one another and what our inner attitude should be. The basic principle is the one of imitation–we treat others imitating the way God treats us. For example, we know God wants us to forgive and not harbor hostility in our hearts. We need to forgive others as He forgives us in Christ. This is a truth that applies to every relationship.

It is important to not only think truth but also to speak truth to one another. God's Word says we are all members of one body. When we are motivated by love and wish someone well, with God's help we will find the time to discuss difficult issues and conflicts. Truth brings freedom and the possibility to heal.

Peace means getting rid of any hostile attitude. To make peace is to get rid of lies, anger, unwholesome talk, bitterness, rage, anger, brawling, and slander, along with every form of malice,

jealousy, and hatred. When we recognize such things in our hearts, we need to be quick to ask and accept forgiveness from God and invite Him to purify our hearts.

The framework and motivation of all our relationships should be sincere love and acceptance of one another. This love involves recognizing and focusing on what is common among us and what connects us. We all have a common origin–we are made in the image and likeness of God. Believers have a common heritage, one common faith, one Lord, one baptism, one Spirit, and one hope to which God has called us, one God and Father of all.

God calls us to look at each other as close relatives and kinsmen, members of God's family. We may not like all our relatives, nor maintain equally close relationships with all, but that does not alter the fact that we are related to them. We are to express this kind of perception externally in showing a kind, gentle, good, respectful, and honoring attitude.

It is impossible to walk in the path of peace and to choose to think or do evil. Strife and hostility are evil. Offense is evil. Revenge is evil. Envy, resentment, and lies are evil. The path of peace means hating what is evil and clinging to what is good. The steps along this path also include helping and meeting needs, hospitality, blessing others, showing sympathy and compassion, and modest thinking.

Written By Hadassah Treu

DAY ONE

ADULTS

In which of your relationships can you be a peacemaker and how?

_____

_____

_____

_____

Today I praise God for...

_____

_____

_____

Today I am confessing...

_____

_____

_____

Today I am praying for...

_____

_____

_____

138

DAY ONE

YOUTH

What does it mean to be a peacemaker?

Today I praise God for...

Today I am confessing...

Today I am praying for...

DAY TWO

ADULTS

What are the concrete steps/actions you can take to be a peacemaker in a problematic relationship?

_____

_____

_____

_____

Today I praise God for...

_____

_____

_____

Today I am confessing...

_____

_____

_____

Today I am praying for...

_____

_____

_____

DAY TWO

YOUTH

What do you think is the most important part of being a peacemaker?

_____

_____

_____

_____

Today I praise God for...

_____

_____

Today I am confessing...

_____

_____

_____

Today I am praying for...

_____

_____

_____

_____

DAY 3 PRAYER

Lord, help us to be
peacemakers
in all our
relationships,
loving others
with Your love.
Help us to focus
on what connects us,
to hate what is evil, and
cling to what is good. Amen.

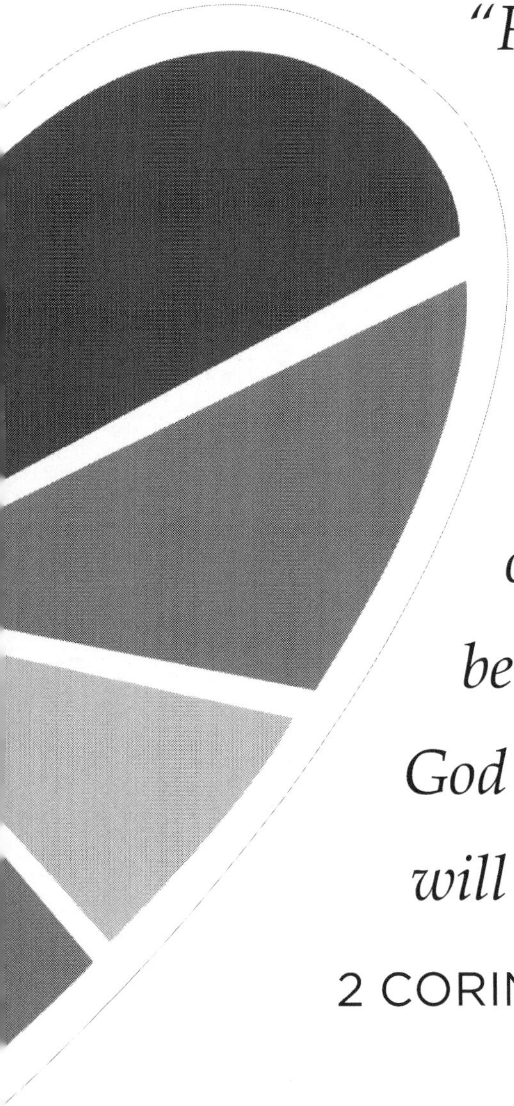

"Finally, brothers and sisters, rejoice.Become mature, be encouraged, be of the same mind, be at peace, and the God of love and peace will be with you."

2 CORINTHIANS 13:11

DAY FOUR

ADULTS

Is there a person whose behavior stirs anger and resentment in you? Why? Could you decide to forgive her/him?

Today I praise God for...

Today I am confessing...

Today I am praying for...

DAY FOUR

YOUTH

Do you have friends or other people with whom you are angry?
Why? Could you decide to forgive her/him?

Today I praise God for...

Today I am confessing...

Today I am praying for...

DAY FIVE

ADULTS

What is the biggest challenge for you in being a peacemaker in your relationships?

_____

_____

_____

_____

Today I praise God for...

_____

_____

_____

Today I am confessing...

_____

_____

_____

Today I am praying for...

_____

_____

_____

146

DAY FIVE

YOUTH

How can you show that you love somebody?

Today I praise God for...

Today I am confessing...

Today I am praying for...

DATE:

147

DAY SIX
ADULTS

What is your definition of being a peacemaker? Write down some attitudes and activities that characterize a peacemaker.

_____
_____
_____
_____

Today I praise God for...

_____
_____
_____

Today I am confessing...

_____
_____
_____

Today I am praying for...

_____
_____
_____

DAY SIX

YOUTH

Why do we need to be kind to one another?

_____

_____

_____

Today I praise God for...

_____

_____

Today I am confessing...

_____

_____

Today I am praying for...

_____

_____

_____

WEEK 11

When Double Standards Challenge Our Faith

"Differing weights and varying measures—both are detestable to the Lord."
(Proverbs 20:10)

Many years ago, I experienced betrayal at the hands of my best friend. It broke my heart and left me wondering if I would ever trust anyone again. I wondered if the bitterness eating away at me would ever give way to forgiveness.

Our Scripture today talks about "differing weights and varying measures." In the days when these words were written, people used stones (weights) and ephahs (measures) to determine cost when buying or selling goods. Often, to increase profit, people found ways to manipulate the system and deceive each other. They used one size stone to determine the weight for buying, but another for selling.

So, what does this Scripture have to do with God's command for us to live justly? He tells us this practice of double standards is detestable to Him. Other Bible translations use the word "abomination." I don't know about you, but that word grabs my attention and convicts me!

Throughout the Bible, we see God does not have double

standards. His command for us to first love Him and then love others is universal. His love isn't dependent upon our race, age, gender, social, or financial class.

This concept of differing weights and measures applies to every aspect of life. Sometimes we carry within us hidden iniquities in judgment, expectation, and behavior. Our subtle habits of gaining a little extra for ourselves become so ingrained, we overlook them. How we view the world and others filters through a lens of life circumstances and the world around us, rather than through the Word of God. What do we expect of others? How deep do our judgments run? Or, is it easy to expect far more from another than we ourselves are ready to give?

But God does not waver in His opinion of double standards. There is no room for them in His Kingdom.

It took me a long time to work through my heartbreak at the hands of my best friend. I had to ask myself some tough questions. Do I expect an apology before I am willing to consider laying down my own bitterness at the feet of Jesus?

I came to realize there would be no justice if my actions were fueled by bitterness and unforgiveness. She never apologized for what she did. But with God's help, I forgave her. I laid down my double standard so I could once again align myself with God's will. And then I found the peace I longed for. The peace that transcends all understanding.

Written By Lori Schumaker

DAY ONE
ADULTS

What double standards are lurking in your life? Ask God to reveal them to you and then write about what He reveals.

Today I praise God for...

Today I am confessing...

Today I am praying for...

DAY ONE

YOUTH

What do you think are some examples of living with double standards for someone your age?

Today I praise God for...

Today I am confessing...

Today I am praying for...

DAY TWO

ADULTS

How have you felt when you have been at the brunt end of a double standard? How did it affect you then and now?

_____

_____

_____

_____

Today I praise God for...

_____

_____

_____

Today I am confessing...

_____

_____

_____

Today I am praying for...

_____

_____

_____

DAY TWO

YOUTH

Have you ever witnessed anyone acting in a way that demonstrated double standards towards others? Talk about the situation.

Today I praise God for...

Today I am confessing...

Today I am praying for...

DAY 3 PRAYER

Dear Father, You are the God of justice. You detest double standards and call us to act justly. Reveal to me, Lord, where double standards may live in my heart. Give me the courage to treat others as I want to be treated, even when it is difficult. In Jesus' name, I pray, Amen.

"I firmly believe a great many prayers are not answered because we are not willing to forgive someone."

D.L. MOODY

DATE:_____

DAY FOUR
ADULTS

If you witnessed injustice in the way of a double-standard, would you be willing to speak truth in love to reconcile the situation?

_____

_____

_____

_____

Today I praise God for...

_____

_____

_____

Today I am confessing...

_____

_____

_____

Today I am praying for...

_____

_____

_____

DAY FOUR

YOUTH

What double standards have you acted upon in the past or even right now?

_____

_____

_____

_____

Today I praise God for...

_____

_____

Today I am confessing...

_____

_____

Today I am praying for...

_____

_____

_____

DAY FIVE
ADULTS

Write a personal prayer asking God to reveal and give you the courage to correct the areas in which you may be acting unjustly.

_____

_____

_____

Today I praise God for...

_____

_____

Today I am confessing...

_____

_____

Today I am praying for...

_____

_____

_____

DAY FIVE
YOUTH

How does carrying anger and bitterness make you feel? How does it get in the way of your life?

_____

_____

_____

_____

Today I praise God for...

_____

_____

Today I am confessing...

_____

_____

Today I am praying for...

_____

_____

_____

_____

161

DAY SIX
ADULTS

What is another example in the Bible of God showing or telling us there are no double standards in His Kingdom?

_____

_____

_____

_____

Today I praise God for...

_____

_____

_____

Today I am confessing...

_____

_____

_____

Today I am praying for...

_____

_____

_____

DATE: _____

DAY SIX

YOUTH

Can you think of a place in the Bible where God treats everyone equally?

_____

_____

_____

Today I praise God for...

_____

_____

Today I am confessing...

_____

_____

Today I am praying for...

_____

_____

_____

WEEK 12

You Are Not an Accident

"I chose you before I formed you in the womb; I set you apart before you were born."
(Jeremiah 1:5a)

Even now I'm sitting and smiling as I think of this passage of Scripture. God knew me before the beginning of time. God knew me, even before He formed me in my mother's womb. Luke 12:7 says that the very hairs on my head are numbered. God knew every single detail about me, including the color of my skin, my gender, the way I would laugh, the color of my eyes, everything! God knew everything and still chose me and made me in His image.

As a part of celebrating black voices and actors, Netflix created the series "Bookmarks: Celebrating Black Voices." I'm not a binge-watcher of anything, but this caught my attention. One of the episodes I was drawn to was Lupita Nyong'o's reading of her book Sulwe. It is a beautiful story of a little girl who was born the color of midnight. The rest of her family had skin tones of dawn, dusk, or high noon, but Sulwe looked nothing like the rest of her family.

As a little girl struggling with her skin tone, she tried everything to get "lighter." She did not believe she fit in because of her skin tone. She thought beauty came from the color of her

skin and prayed God would make her the color of daylight.

After a conversation with her mom, she was reminded of what her name meant. Sulwe meant Star. Stars brighten up a night sky. She was reminded that beauty came from the inside, but she was still not convinced.

That night a shooting star came to find Sulwe and told her a story of Day and Night. Sulwe realized that both Day and Night were important, each had their respective purposes. While Day was good for working and playing, Night was what allowed people to rest and rejuvenate so they could continue playing and working during the day.

As Sulwe finally realized her importance, her attitude towards herself began to change. She understood she was no accident, and true beauty was not reflected in the color of her skin.

The Bible is very clear that God made us in His image. "Then God said, 'Let us make man in our image, according to our likeness. They will rule the fish of the sea, the birds of the sky, the livestock, the whole earth, and the creatures that crawl on the earth.' So God created man in his own image; he created him in the image of God; he created them male and female" (Genesis 1:26-27).

We are made in God's beautiful image, and all ranges of skin tone are beautiful to Him. Let us not forget that whenever we look at ourselves or others.

Written By Kaysian C. Gordon

DAY ONE
ADULTS

What is one thing that stood out about this story?

_____

_____

_____

_____

Today I praise God for...

_____

_____

_____

Today I am confessing...

_____

_____

_____

Today I am praying for...

_____

_____

_____

DAY ONE

YOUTH

What is one thing that you liked about this story?

Today I praise God for...

Today I am confessing...

Today I am praying for...

DAY TWO

ADULTS

Can you see yourself in Sulwe?

_____
_____
_____
_____

Today I praise God for...

_____
_____
_____

Today I am confessing...

_____
_____
_____

Today I am praying for...

_____
_____
_____
_____

DAY TWO

YOUTH

Do you think Sulwe is beautiful? Why?

_____

_____

_____

_____

Today I praise God for...

_____

_____

Today I am confessing...

_____

_____

Today I am praying for...

_____

_____

_____

DAY 3 PRAYER

Dear Heavenly Father, thank You that we are not on this earth by accident or coincidence. You have chosen us to be born for a time such as now and for us to walk in our purpose with love and unity among all people, not based on our skin tone.

"*Every aspect of the way God views and saves sinners is designed to undermine racism and lead to a reconciled and redeemed humanity from every people group in the world.*"

JOHN PIPER

BLOODLINES: RACE, CROSS, AND THE CHRISTIAN

DAY FOUR
ADULTS

Do you have trouble accepting the way you look on the outside?

Today I praise God for...

Today I am confessing...

Today I am praying for...

DAY FOUR

YOUTH

Are you concerned about the way others view you?

Today I praise God for...

Today I am confessing...

Today I am praying for...

DAY FIVE

ADULTS

What is one thing about your physical appearance that you love?

_____

_____

_____

_____

Today I praise God for...

_____

_____

_____

Today I am confessing...

_____

_____

_____

Today I am praying for...

_____

_____

_____

DAY FIVE
YOUTH

What is one thing about your physical appearance that you love?

_____

_____

_____

Today I praise God for...

_____

_____

Today I am confessing...

_____

_____

Today I am praying for...

_____

_____

_____

DATE: _____

DAY SIX

ADULTS

What are some non-physical characteristics that make you unique?

_____

_____

_____

Today I praise God for...

_____

_____

Today I am confessing...

_____

_____

Today I am praying for...

_____

_____

_____

DAY SIX

YOUTH

What about your personality makes you unique?

_____

_____

_____

_____

Today I praise God for...

_____

_____

Today I am confessing...

_____

_____

Today I am praying for...

_____

_____

_____

WEEK 13

Becoming One of the Family

"When the time came to completion, God sent his Son, born of a woman, born under the law, to redeem those under the law, so that we might receive adoption as sons." (Galatians 4:4-5)

Everyone has a desire to fit in, be recognized, or have access to particular resources. C.S. Lewis writes in his book, The Weight of Glory, a fascinating essay on the dangers of trying to make it into the inner circle of groups or organizations but we still find ourselves striving to be "on the inside". Truth be told, there are few groups truly open to all people and give access to all resources for the entire group. One place you do have access to everything is in the family of God.

If we look at this passage of Scripture carefully what we notice is that God's family is orchestrated by God according to His plan. The phrase "When the time came to completion" indicates that God had a plan for sending His son, Jesus Christ, into the world to redeem humanity. You could understand Genesis 3- Revelation 22 as God's plan for reconciling a broken relationship with humanity. The adoption taking place in the above passage is a reminder that God's plans are not always ours and nothing we do can ever thwart His plans.

We are also told that Jesus lived a life like ours. He experienced

life in much the same way we do. However, Jesus is not like us. He obeyed the law perfectly and by obeying the law and living perfectly, dying, and rising from the dead, He provides redemption to all humanity.

What is the purpose for all this? Paul answers, "So that we might receive adoption as sons." Through the redemption that is offered and found in Christ, all people have the opportunity to be adopted into God's family.

We had the privilege of adopting our first child recently. Through all the joy of having a brand-new baby in the family, the greatest day came on the day of our adoption finalization. In front of some of our friends and family, a judge declared that little girl a member of our family. The judge stated she had all the rights and privileges that any child biologically born to us would have. Friend, when you become a member of God's family you are adopted into His family and nothing can change that.

Adoption into the family of God should cause all Christians to understand the implications for the way that we should treat others. When I recognize that those who claim the name of Christ are adopted into our family, I should guard the way I treat them. This means that when someone puts down my brother or sister in Christ because of their ethnicity, race, or gender, I should be quick to jump in and help them. The body of Christ should look after its fellow family members and not seek to harm them because we understand they are a part of God's family, and He has graciously adopted both of us into His family.

Written By David Botts

DAY ONE

ADULTS

How can you overcome the temptation to think that you deserve to be adopted into the family of God?

_____

_____

_____

Today I praise God for...

_____

_____

_____

Today I am confessing...

_____

_____

_____

Today I am praying for...

_____

_____

_____

DAY ONE
YOUTH

How can you thank God today for adopting you into His family?

_____

Today I praise God for...

_____

Today I am confessing...

_____

Today I am praying for...

_____

DAY TWO

ADULTS

Where in your life are you not trusting in God's timing or plan for what He is accomplishing in and through you?

_____

_____

_____

_____

Today I praise God for...

_____

_____

_____

Today I am confessing...

_____

_____

_____

Today I am praying for...

_____

_____

_____

DAY TWO

YOUTH

What do we learn about who God is from this passage?

_____

_____

_____

_____

Today I praise God for...

_____

_____

Today I am confessing...

_____

_____

Today I am praying for...

_____

_____

_____

_____

DAY 3
PRAYER

*God, please help me
to see people the
way You see
them. Help me
to recognize
the privilege of
what it means
to be adopted into
Your family, and
help me to not take
the adoption I never
deserved for granted.*

"Adoption would become a priority in our churches if our churches themselves saw our brotherhood and sisterhood in the church itself rather than in our fleshly identities."

RUSSELL D. MOORE
ADOPTED FOR LIFE: THE
PRIORITY OF ADOPTION
FOR CHRISTIAN FAMILIES &
CHURCHES

DAY FOUR

ADULTS

Do you have reservations about certain people becoming a part of the family of God? If yes, how does this passage correct you?

_____

_____

_____

Today I praise God for...

_____

_____

Today I am confessing...

_____

_____

Today I am praying for...

_____

_____

_____

DAY FOUR

YOUTH

Jesus is like us in the way He was born and the way He had to live.
Why is this a good thing?

_____

_____

_____

Today I praise God for...

_____

_____

_____

Today I am confessing...

_____

_____

_____

Today I am praying for...

_____

_____

_____

DAY FIVE
ADULTS

How might you thank God today for adopting you into His family?

_____

_____

_____

Today I praise God for...

_____

_____

Today I am confessing...

_____

_____

Today I am praying for...

_____

_____

_____

DAY FIVE
YOUTH

Jesus is not like us in how He actually lived his life (He lived a perfect life). Why is this a good thing?

_____

_____

_____

_____

Today I praise God for...

_____

_____

Today I am confessing...

_____

_____

Today I am praying for...

_____

_____

_____

DAY SIX

ADULTS

Who can you share this good news with in the next few days?

_____

_____

_____

Today I praise God for...

_____

_____

Today I am confessing...

_____

_____

Today I am praying for...

_____

_____

_____

DAY SIX

YOUTH

What questions do you have from reading this passage?

Today I praise God for...

Today I am confessing...

Today I am praying for...

WEEK 14

Love as Jesus Loves

"Dear friends, let us love one another, because love is from God, and everyone who loves has been born of God and knows God. The one who does not love does not know God, because God is love."
(1 John 4:7-8)

As children, we learn the song "Jesus Loves the Little Children." It teaches some key points. One is that Jesus died for all. During this time of civil unrest and battles across the races, we need to remember that Jesus died for all. John 3:16 says, "For God loved the world in this way: He gave his one and only Son, so that everyone who believes in him will not perish but have eternal life." What a gift!

God shows His love for us repeatedly. 1 John 4:7-8 and Isaiah 54:10 are just a couple. These verses speak of God's undying love for His children; however, when you watch the news, you get a deep sense of sadness and think God's love is not evident to those around us.

I am discouraged when I see neighbors calling the police on innocent people because of their skin color or when I see children banned from playing with others because of their

192

race. It can be a lot to process.

I am a black girl raised in the South, and my father and mother raised me to love everybody. My grandfather is 101, and he, too, taught me we are all equal at the cross of Jesus.

I followed their lead teaching my daughters to love and respect others. What I failed to teach them is that hate is real, and people may hate them without knowing the content of their character. I failed to teach them what to say when others plot against them because they look different. I failed to teach them what to do when they are called names.

I am thankful God gave me a new day to correct my mistake. This year, I taught my daughters no matter what others do to you, God desires for us not to reciprocate hate for hate. When faced with hate from others. We need to choose to trust God and His Word.

We must teach our children that God is love—He does not only love us when we are good; He also loves us when we are not. The only way this world will ever be different is if each of us makes it our business to show love. We do not always have to agree, but we can disagree in love. God is love. Lesson learned.

Written By Paula Sanders Blackwell

DAY ONE

ADULTS

What did your parents teach you about love?

_____

_____

_____

Today I praise God for...

_____

_____

Today I am confessing...

_____

_____

Today I am praying for...

_____

_____

_____

DAY ONE
YOUTH

What did your parents teach you about loving others?

_____

_____

_____

_____

Today I praise God for...

_____

_____

Today I am confessing...

_____

_____

Today I am praying for...

_____

_____

_____

DAY TWO

ADULTS

When is the first time you saw hate?

_____
_____
_____

_____

Today I praise God for...

_____
_____

_____

Today I am confessing...

_____
_____

_____

Today I am praying for...

_____
_____

_____

DAY TWO

YOUTH

Do you understand what it means to be a friend?

Today I praise God for...

Today I am confessing...

Today I am praying for...

DAY 3 PRAYER

God, please help us learn to love each other as You love us. Help us to gain an understanding of Your will for our lives. Bring us closer to Your love and peace. Give us the will and passion to search our hearts so we can begin healing our nation. Give us love from the Father to see each other with loving eyes, eyes that don't see color but hearts. In the matchless name of Jesus, Amen.

"Our love to God is measured by our everyday fellowship with others and the love it displays."

ANDREW MURRAY

DAY FOUR

ADULTS

Why do you think the nation is in disarray over race?

_____

_____

_____

_____

Today I praise God for...

_____

_____

_____

Today I am confessing...

_____

_____

_____

Today I am praying for...

_____

_____

_____

_____

DATE: _____

DAY FOUR

YOUTH

Do you think the color of a person's skin is important?

_____
_____
_____
_____

Today I praise God for...

_____
_____

Today I am confessing...

_____
_____

Today I am praying for...

_____
_____
_____

DAY FIVE
ADULTS

Why is the need to be right so prevalent?

Today I praise God for...

Today I am confessing...

Today I am praying for...

DAY FIVE

YOUTH

Do you think God notices when we are different colors on the outside?

Today I praise God for...

Today I am confessing...

Today I am praying for...

DAY SIX
ADULTS

How can you be an example to your children teaching them how to treat people?

_____

_____

_____

_____

Today I praise God for...

_____

_____

_____

Today I am confessing...

_____

_____

_____

Today I am praying for...

_____

_____

_____

DAY SIX

YOUTH

How do you think God feels when you befriend those who might look different from you?

_____

_____

_____

Today I praise God for...

_____

_____

Today I am confessing...

_____

_____

Today I am praying for...

_____

_____

_____

WEEK 15

I Didn't Know...

"Rescue those being taken off to death, and save those stumbling toward slaughter. If you say, 'But we didn't know about this,' won't he who weighs hearts consider it? Won't he who protects your life know? Won't he repay a person according to his work?"
(Proverbs 24:11-12)

Is there anything as frustrating as someone who excuses inaction by saying they didn't know? "I didn't know I had to do the work today." Or "I didn't know you wanted it now." Or, "Wait is that what you meant? I didn't know that, sorry."

I think what makes this frustrating is that a lot of people use the statement "I didn't know" in place of the truth. The truth usually is along the lines of "I didn't do it because I didn't really want to" or "I didn't do it because it just wasn't that important to me." The truth doesn't sound quite as nice, does it?

However, we should all be aware that there will come a time when "I didn't know" will not be a valid excuse. "I didn't think I could do anything" won't matter as an excuse either. Because the bottom line with excuses is this, God knew all along. And He knows whether or not you knew too.

When I think of all the injustices taking place, it's jarring. What's even more unsettling is the number of Christians who feel

it's not "their place" to speak out and say anything. Another sad thing is that many have still not felt the need for self-reflection either. In fact, there has been what seems to be a comfort in knowing that "at least I didn't do it."

It's easy to ignore things when you aren't directly involved. But as a Christian, it should be different. If those excuses don't work today, they certainly won't work on Judgment Day. Do we honestly think that God, who knows all, will be satisfied with us doing nothing at this time? Will He approve of His children doing nothing to speak up or help others that are suffering from injustice? Will He really accept our excuses and inaction?

The above Scripture says we should rescue those unjustly sentenced to die, and that God knows whether or not we knew what was going on. God is not pleased with His children turning a blind eye to injustice just because it doesn't personally affect them. He's not pleased when His children pretend they didn't know about injustice. He's not pleased when we make excuses for not defending others

It also says that God will repay all people as their actions deserve. This could be good news or bad news. Remember, inaction is an active choice.

So ask yourself, is knowing and not doing, something you want to be rewarded for by God?

Written By Chanel Moore

DAY ONE
ADULTS

Do you feel you have a responsibility to speak out for those who have been treated unjustly?

_____

_____

_____

Today I praise God for...

_____

_____

Today I am confessing...

_____

_____

Today I am praying for...

_____

_____

_____

DAY ONE
YOUTH

Do you feel you should say something when you see others being treated unfairly?

_____

_____

_____

_____

Today I praise God for...

_____

_____

Today I am confessing...

_____

_____

Today I am praying for...

_____

_____

_____

DAY TWO
ADULTS

Why do you think it's scary to speak up?

_____

_____

_____

_____

Today I praise God for...

_____

_____

Today I am confessing...

_____

_____

Today I am praying for...

_____

_____

_____

DAY TWO

YOUTH

Do you feel nervous about speaking up for someone who hasn't been able to speak for themselves?

_____

_____

_____

Today I praise God for...

_____

_____

Today I am confessing...

_____

_____

Today I am praying for...

_____

_____

_____

DAY 3
PRAYER

Lord, thank You for hating injustice and mistreatment of Your creation. Please stir within us the desire to love justice as You do. Give us a heart for all of Your creation. Forgive us if we've ever excused injustice because it didn't directly hurt us and give us the ability to fight against it for Your glory. Help us to love one another. We all matter to You; help us to treat one another that way. In Jesus' name, Amen.

"If thou art wise thou knowest thine own ignorance; and thou art ignorant if thou knowest not thyself."

MARTIN LUTHER

DAY FOUR

How do you think God feels about that injustice taking place?

_____

_____

_____

_____

Today I praise God for...

_____

_____

_____

Today I am confessing...

_____

_____

_____

Today I am praying for...

_____

_____

_____

DAY FOUR

YOUTH

How do you think God feels about the people you see hurting?

Today I praise God for...

Today I am confessing...

Today I am praying for...

DAY FIVE

ADULTS

How do you think God feels about how you respond to injustice?

_____

_____

_____

Today I praise God for...

_____

_____

Today I am confessing...

_____

_____

Today I am praying for...

_____

_____

_____

DAY FIVE

YOUTH

How do you think God feels about how you treat others?

_____

_____

_____

_____

Today I praise God for...

_____

_____

Today I am confessing...

_____

_____

Today I am praying for...

_____

_____

_____

DAY SIX

ADULTS

DATE: _____

Is there something practical you can do today to seek justice for others?

_____

_____

_____

Today I praise God for...

_____

_____

Today I am confessing...

_____

_____

Today I am praying for...

_____

_____

_____

218

DAY SIX

YOUTH

How can you help somebody today?

Today I praise God for...

Today I am confessing...

Today I am praying for...

WEEK 16

Through Jesus' Eyes

"As Jesus went on from there, he saw a man named Matthew sitting at the tax office, and he said to him, 'Follow me,' so he got up and followed him."
(Matthew 9:9)

For Jesus to call Matthew, a tax collector, was a big deal. In Jesus' time, tax collectors were viewed as traitors, Jews who had turned against their own people to help the Romans with their continued oppression. They often became rich by overtaxing the Jews and taking the money for themselves. Tax collectors were reviled by the Jews.

Not only did calling Matthew not go over well with the other disciples, it definitely did not go over well with the Pharisees. Once Jesus called Matthew and he accepted, they gathered at his home for a dinner party. This was where the Pharisees found them and made their objections known.

"While he was reclining at the table in the house, many tax collectors and sinners came as guests to eat with Jesus and His disciples. When the Pharisees saw this, they asked His disciples, "Why does your Teacher eat with tax collectors and sinners?"
(Matthew 9:10-11)

What I love so much about this story, and about Jesus, is that He doesn't care about their objections. He knows there is

opposition between Jews and tax collectors. He knows how tax collectors are viewed by others. He knows that spending time with sinners is the unpopular choice. He's not interested in any of this; He's only interested in saving souls. I love His response to them:

"But when He heard this, He said, 'Those who are well do not need a doctor, but those who are sick do. Go and learn what this means: I desire mercy and not sacrifice. For I didn't come to call the righteous, but sinners.'" (Matthew 9:12-13)

As I look at this story and Jesus' response, I try to apply this to my own life. Right now in our country, there is a lot of political and social unrest. We're letting our differences, whether it be race, gender, sexuality, political affiliation, religious beliefs, or more, divide our nation.

What if I stopped focusing on what makes us different and focus on what we have in common? What if I looked at others through the eyes of Jesus?

Imagine if we started viewing others as Jesus did? Instead of focusing on differences, we made a point to look at others through eyes of love and acceptance. What an impact we could make!

The Bible states, a house divided will fall (Mark 3:25). Division gets us nowhere. The only way to survive and defeat all the "isms" (racism, sexism, etc.) is to instead seek unity.

"How good and pleasant it is when brothers live together in harmony!" (Psalm 133:1)

Written By Alexis Newlin

DAY ONE
ADULTS

How can I create more diversity in my relationships?

_____

_____

_____

Today I praise God for...

_____

_____

_____

Today I am confessing...

_____

_____

_____

Today I am praying for...

_____

_____

_____

DAY ONE
YOUTH

Do I hang out with others that look different than me? If not, why?

_____

_____

_____

Today I praise God for...

_____

_____

Today I am confessing...

_____

_____

Today I am praying for...

_____

_____

_____

DAY TWO

ADULTS

Do I engage in conversations with others that believe differently than I do?

_____

_____

_____

_____

Today I praise God for...

_____

_____

_____

Today I am confessing...

_____

_____

_____

Today I am praying for...

_____

_____

_____

_____

DAY TWO

YOUTH

How do I talk to others that have different beliefs than me?

_____

_____

_____

_____

Today I praise God for...

_____

_____

Today I am confessing...

_____

_____

Today I am praying for...

_____

_____

_____

_____

DAY 3
PRAYER

God, thank You for creating us each so differently. Help us find a way to live in peace despite these differences and to find a way to connect with others. May we seek out unity and see others as Christ does. Amen.

"For we were all baptized by one Spirit into one body — whether Jews or Greeks, whether slaves or free — and we were all given one Spirit to drink."

1 CORINTHIANS 12:13

DAY FOUR

ADULTS

What part can I do to bring unity to my community?

Today I praise God for...

Today I am confessing...

Today I am praying for...

DAY FOUR

YOUTH

How can I bring people together that are different?

Today I praise God for...

Today I am confessing...

Today I am praying for...

DAY FIVE

ADULTS

Have you ever felt like an outcast? How did it feel?

_____

_____

_____

_____

Today I praise God for...

_____

_____

_____

Today I am confessing...

_____

_____

_____

Today I am praying for...

_____

_____

_____

_____

DAY FIVE
YOUTH

Have you ever felt left out with friends? How did it feel?

Today I praise God for...

Today I am confessing...

Today I am praying for...

31

DAY SIX

ADULTS

How would your life change if you viewed others as Jesus did?

_____

_____

_____

_____

Today I praise God for...

_____

_____

Today I am confessing...

_____

_____

Today I am praying for...

_____

_____

_____

DAY SIX

YOUTH

How can you view others through Jesus' eyes?

_____

_____

_____

Today I praise God for...

_____

_____

Today I am confessing...

_____

_____

Today I am praying for...

_____

_____

_____

Endnotes

1   Steven Rose, "Darwin, Race, and Gender," National Center for Biotechnology, 2009, https://www.ncbi.nlm.nih.gov/pmc/articles/PMC2672903/, accessed 7-31-20

2   Phil Moore, "What Your Biology Teacher Didn't Tell You About Darwin," 2017, https://www.thegospelcoalition.org/article/what-your-biology-teacher-didnt-tell-you-about-charles-darwin/, accessed 7-31-20

ABOUT THE AUTHORS

Donna E. Lane, Ph.D.

Dr. Donna E. Lane is an award-winning author, professor of counseling, and Christian Counselor. She is also the founder of the Cody Lane Foundation, which provides individual and small group discipleship and Christian education.

🐦 @Doctordelane

📷 @doctordelane

f @dr.donna.e.lane

http://www.doctordlane.com/

🐦 @faithe_bennett

📷 @walk.by.faithe

f @faithe.elizabeth

https://faithebennett.wixsite.com/website

Faithe Bennett

Currently, Faithe is finishing her undergraduate degree in Biblical Counseling at Spurgeon College. She also works for Spurgeon College and Midwestern Baptist Theological Seminary as an Admissions Representative and is interning with the ACBC.

Gina Barton Sewell

I am a wife, mom, and grandma. I love to encourage others in their walk with the Lord. I write about my journey on my website. In my free time, I like serving in my church and community and spending time with my amazing family.

🐦 @ginabartonsewell

📷 @spikeswife18

f @gina.meredith.5

www.ginabartonsewell.wordpress.com

Nicholas Tim Murphy

Nicholas Murphy is a graduate of Baptist Bible College. He is currently working on his Masters of Divinity at Liberty University.

@nmurphy802

@nickmurphy10

@nicholasmurphy8

@bryonm

@bryonmondok

@bryon.mondok

http://www.bryonmondok.com/

Bryon Mondok

Bryon Mondok is a digital engagement practitioner, mission's pastor, and former missionary. He loves to write, read, play guitar, ride his mountain bike, and run. He lives by the mantra, "You're not living until you give your life away."

Gary David Flamberg

Gary is a contributing author to Devotable as well as Christian Devotions and Bayside Devotional. He is a Jesus-follower and a fellow sojourner whose desire is to: pursue God passionately, represent Him boldly and accurately, and encourage others to do likewise.

@garydavid.flamberg.5

@crystal_a_dixon

@cdadixon

http://crystaladixon.com/

Crystal A. Dixon

Crystal is a Bible teacher and Christian writer. She encourages others to seek and nurture a relationship with Jesus and realize their identity in Christ. In her spare time, Crystal enjoys the beach and reading. She and her husband, Donald, live in North Carolina.

ABOUT THE AUTHORS

Dr. Natalie H. Ragland

Natalie H. Ragland is a veterinarian, mentor, and author of the year-long devotional book Encourage Yourself in the Lord which initially began as a journey to deepen her relationship with God.

🐦 @completeyourcalling

📷 @NatalieRagland3

f @completeyourcalling

http://www.completeyourcalling. blog

Vicki Bentley

📷 @purposeful_joy

f @the.joyful.journey

https://purposefuljoy. wordpress.com/

A Scottish native, Vicki now calls Upstate New York home. As a writer and editor, she loves to encourage women to pursue Jesus-centered, joy-filled living in the gloriously hard and wonderful trenches of motherhood and adulthood.

Hadassah Treu

Hadassah is a Christian blogger and author, a bilingual poet, and a marketing specialist. Her passion is to encourage people to stand firm in the faith, to grow spiritually, and to know and apply Biblical truths to their lives.

🐦 @onthewaybg

📷 @hadassahtreu

f @onthewaybg

https://onthewaybg.com/

Lori Schumaker

As a wife, mom, teacher, and more, Lori's heart is to encourage others to meet the challenges of life with the hope of Christ. In her book she weaves lessons on letting go and living surrendered to Jesus by telling her family's adoption story.

🐦 @lori_schumaker

📷 @lori_schumaker

f @searchingformoments

http://www.lorischumaker.com/

📷 @kaysigordon

f @kaysian.gordon

www.kaysigordon.com/

Kaysian C. Gordon

Kaysian Gordon is a mother, financial advisor, author, writer, speaker, and Bible teacher. After years of education in the financial arena, Kaysian felt the call to start writing a faith blog. She also guest blogs for Recraft Devotional Group, a group dedicated to recrafting lives.

David Botts

I am a staff pastor at Crossway Baptist Church in Springfield, MO. I am married to Jess and we have one daughter, Harper. I blog infrequently at workingtheologian.com, and I enjoy watching anything to do with the Iowa Hawkeyes, playing golf, talking about theology, and reading books.

🐦 @bottsman

📷 @bottsman

f @david.m.botts

https://workingtheologian.com/

🐦 @Redellswife

📷 @paulaprinciples

f @paulaprinciples

www.paulablackwell.com

Paula Blackwell Sanders

I am a native of Birmingham, AL. I currently live in Savannah, GA. I am the wife of Redell Blackwell, the love of my life. Our lives began in 2014 so we are still newlyweds. Together we merged four kids and a dog. I am an educator and entrepreneur. I am a Bible teacher and I love to sing.

ABOUT THE AUTHORS

Chanel Moore

Chanel Moore is a teacher who enjoys writing. Her newest book is D.A.U.G.H.T.E.R.S., which focuses on what it means to be the daughter of a loving, Heavenly Father. In addition to writing, she does a one-minute Bible study called Study this Book.

@nellyacc

@nellyacc

@avril.cobb

https://chanelcobb.wordpress.com/

@brave_podcast

@apeachinfresno

@apeachincali

www.apeachincali.com

Alexis Newlin

Alexis is a 37-year-old lover of Jesus, loose leaf tea, roller coasters, writing stories, and going on adventures. Originally from Marietta, GA, she now resides in Fresno, CA. She currently writes for several online ministries and launched her first podcast, The Brave Podcast.

Thank you so much for reading one of our devotional books. If you like what we're doing and want to read more, please take a look at our other devotional books and journals by visiting our website at https://devotableapp.com

If you like these types of books and devotionals, we'd love for you to take a look at our other journal and devotional *"Prayer: Approaching the Throne of Grace"*.

Having a victorious prayer life doesn't have to be a dream. You can study what God's Word says about prayer and learn how to connect with God daily. This books is perfect for individual journaling or a group Bible study through prayer. It features:

- 6x9 trim size with plenty of room to write
- An open journaling page at the end of each work for your reflections
- Guided questions each day helping you write about that week's devotion topic
- A beautiful layout growing with you as you journal through the week

Learn more about Devotable at https://devotableapp.com